instant gratification
ornaments

instant gratification
ornaments

FAST & FABULOUS PROJECTS

by Genevieve A. Sterbenz | Photography by Julie Toy

CHRONICLE BOOKS
SAN FRANCISCO

Copyright © 2001 Genevieve A. Sterbenz. Photography copyright © 2001 by Julie Toy. Illustrations copyright © 2001 by Nicole Kaufman. All rights reserved. No part of this book may be reproduced in any form without written permission from the publisher.

Library of Congress Cataloging-in-Publication Data available.

ISBN: 0-8118-3023-3

Printed in Hong Kong

Designed by Level, Calistoga, CA
Typesetting by Level, Calistoga, CA
Prop Styling by Gia Russo

The author would like to acknowledge ScottiCrafts for their contribution
and she would also like to thank Lizette LaForge for all her help.
The photographer would like to thank Nancy Sullivan, Tracy Richell,
Jenny Roberts, Becky Rosetti, and Chrissy Hargrove.

Mod Podge is a registered trademark of Plaid Enterprises, Inc.
Styrofoam is a registered trademark of the Dow Chemical Company.
Teenie Weenie Beadies is a registered trademark of ScottiCrafts, a division of Tape Systems, Inc.
Ultimate Bond Tape is a registered trademark of ScottiCrafts, a division of Tape Systems, Inc.
X-Acto Knife is a registered trademark of X-Acto Crescent Products, Inc.

Distributed in Canada by Raincoast Books
9050 Shaughnessy Street
Vancouver, British Columbia V6P 6E5

10 9 8 7 6 5 4 3 2 1

Chronicle Books LLC
85 Second Street
San Francisco, California 94105

www.chroniclebooks.com

This book is intended as a guide to the craft of ornament-making. As with any craft project, it is important that all the instructions are followed carefully, as failure to do so could result in injury. Every effort has been made to present the information in this book in a clear, complete, and accurate manner, however not every situation can be anticipated and there can be no substitute for common sense. Check product labels, for example, to make sure that the materials you use are safe and nontoxic. The authors and Chronicle Books disclaim any and all liability resulting from injuries or damage caused during the production or use of the ornaments discussed in this book.

FOR TOM,

who is my best friend, my true love, and my biggest blessing.

Merry Christmas.

All my love,

GENEVIEVE

table of

contents

introduction

Little compares to the joy and splendor of a decorated Christmas tree. From the moment the tree is brought home and placed in its stand to the unwrapping of the last ornament before it is placed on the tree, we re-experience every Christmas that has gone before.

Instant Gratification: Ornaments offers a collection of forty designs for making beautiful, original ornaments to hang from the boughs of your tree, regardless of your previous craft experience. Every project comes with step-by-step instructions, is illustrated with full-color photographs, and has been thoroughly tested to ensure simple and foolproof techniques.

Whether you are decorating a tree that stretches to the ceiling or something a bit more humble, you are sure to notice the special details that characterize each ornament. Frosted glass balls with holiday words in relief are reminiscent of a windowpane on a cold, snowy winter's morning, and jingle bells clustered to look like grapes and paper bells made from antique sheet music serve to remind you of the sonorous spirit of the season. You will find magnificent ways to soften the glow of tiny lights by placing them in a sleeve of gossamer organdy or adorning them with bows of pink cellophane. Ideas for ornaments, lighting, and garlands will allow you to decorate your tree from top to bottom.

Don't stop when you've finished creating a festive tree. Arrange decorated frosted-collar mini-lights on your mantel, place a snow-covered pinecone in icy blue at each place setting at your table, or tuck a gift for a friend in a small, embossed velvet pouch with a personal monogram. These little works of art will shine with the holiday spirit and bring you cherished memories in Christmases to come.

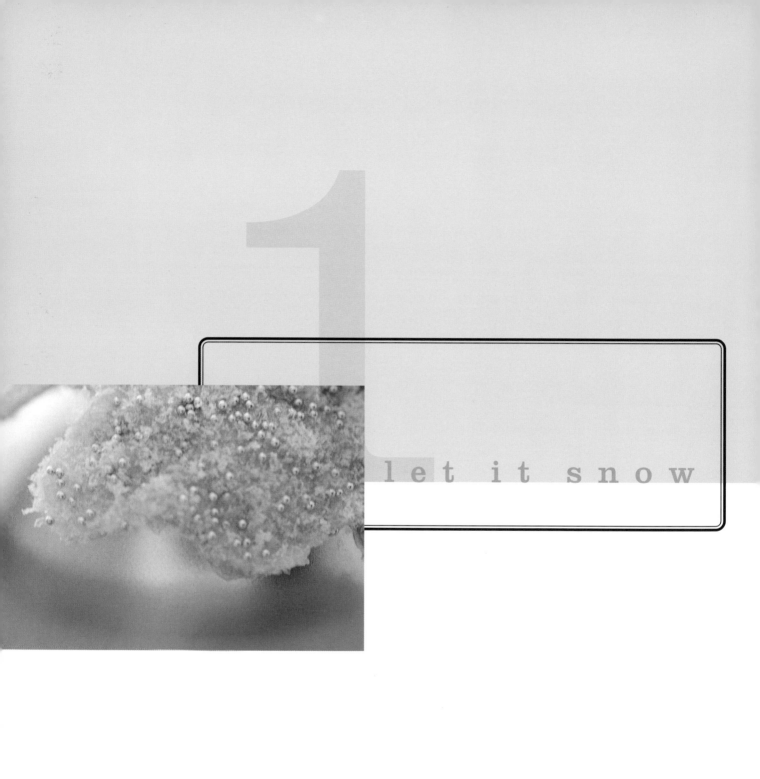

1

let it snow

Silver-Blue Snowbird

An ordinary little plastic bird can be transformed into a sparkling ornament by covering it with glitter and rhinestones. Nestle your snowbird into a white feather nest and give it a home among the branches of a fragrant pine tree.

YOU WILL NEED:

Kraft paper

Plastic-coated Styrofoam bird with
    feathers and wire stem, 5 inches
    long from head to tail

6-inch-square Styrofoam block

High-tack white glue

Sponge brush

Fine glitter in silver

1 package (144 count) 3 mm
    flat-backed rhinestones in turquoise

1 package (144 count) 6 mm flat-backed
    rhinestones in turquoise

Straightedge ruler (optional)

Wire cutters (optional)

30-gauge wire in silver (optional)

10 to 15 feathers in white (optional)

1. Cover clean, flat work surface with kraft paper. Set wire end of bird into Styrofoam block and place on work surface.

2. Apply thin layer of glue to surface area of bird using sponge brush. Sprinkle glitter over glued area until covered. Let glue dry completely.

3. Apply dab of glue to back of 3 mm rhinestone using nozzle of glue bottle. Position and press at base of beak. Add rhinestones around base of beak and on head. Do not apply rhinestones to beak, feet, or underside of tail.

4. Working from head to tail, glue, position, and press 3 mm rhinestones on body of bird; use 6 mm rhinestones for wings and breast area. Let glue dry completely.

5. To make optional nest, use ruler and wire cutters to measure and cut a 12-inch piece of wire. Hold a feather in left hand with stem pointing to the right. Wrap one end of wire twice around stem. Do not cut wire. Position second feather, with stem pointing to right, on top of and farther to the right of first feather. Wrap with wire to secure. Continue overlapping and wiring feathers to create a feather garland. When desired length is achieved, bring two end feathers together, overlapping them. Secure with wire. Using wire cutters, trim end of wire. Place bird in nest.

Glitter Collars for Mini-Lights

With a little glitter and some glue, you can create the luminescent effect of newly fallen snow on store-bought mini-lights. Display the lights on your tree or string them across your holiday table as a centerpiece. Be sure to read the caution note below before using your collars.

YOU WILL NEED:

Cookie sheet

Kitchen aluminum foil

Strand of mini-lights in white with
   removable plastic collars

Fine glitter in warm highlight

Small bowl

#4 natural-bristle paintbrush

High-tack white glue

Teaspoon

CAUTION: Never use mini-lights that have leave covered lights on unattended.

1. Cover cookie sheet with aluminum foil.

2. Remove a collar from a mini-light and place on cookie sheet.

3. Pour glitter into bowl and set aside.

4. Using paintbrush, apply thin coat of glue to outside of collar.

5. Holding collar over bowl, use teaspoon to sprinkle glitter onto glued area. Rotate collar to cover all sides. Set on cookie sheet and let glue dry completely.

6. Repeat steps 2 through 5 for remaining collars. Do not glue and glitter inside the collars.

7. Place collars over mini-lights.

CAUTION: Never use mini-lights that have broken or cracked sockets, are frayed, are missing bulbs, or have loose or exposed wires. Doing so may cause electric shock or start a fire. Do not leave covered lights on unattended.

Ice-Blue Snowflakes

Remember cutting out paper snowflakes as a child? This old favorite is given new life in two shades of vellum, accented with rhinestones. Place these ornaments near lights on a tree and see how the vellum creates a hazy glow in shades of blue. Or display the snowflakes at different heights on a window and let the sun create the same effect.

YOU WILL NEED:

Straightedge ruler

#1 pencil

2 sheets of vellum, 1 in aqua
   and 1 in deep blue

Scissors

Snowflake pattern (page 103)

Tracing paper

Dry ballpoint pen

High-tack white glue

Two 3 mm flat-backed rhinestones,
   1 in aqua and 1 in deep blue

Matching thread in aqua and deep blue

Hand-sewing needle

1. Using ruler and pencil, measure and mark a 3-inch square on aqua vellum. Cut out with scissors. Fold square in half vertically, bringing left edge over to meet right edge. Then bring bottom edge up to meet top edge. Set square aside while retaining folded position. Folds should be on bottom and left edge.

2. Use pencil to trace snowflake pattern on page 103 on tracing paper.

3. Lay pattern, penciled-side down, on folded vellum square and use dry ballpoint pen to trace over pencil lines, pressing down firmly to transfer lines. Lift tracing paper from square. There should be a faint pencil pattern on the vellum. Retrace pattern lines in pencil if necessary.

4. Cut along marked lines. Open folded snowflake.

5. Use nozzle on glue bottle to add dab of glue to back side of aqua rhinestone. Position and adhere to center of snowflake.

6. Using ruler and scissors, measure and cut 12 inches of thread. Thread needle and pull to midpoint. Tie ends in double knot. Pierce snowflake at a top stem with needle. Pull thread to midpoint and cut free from needle. Tie thread in double knot at top to make loop. Trim ends.

7. Repeat steps 1 through 6 for snowflake in deep blue.

Beaded Icicle

The simple beauty and elegance of this ornament is matched only by how easy it is to make. Beads in graduating sizes are strung together to mimic a glistening icicle. Before you go out and buy beads, take a look through your costume jewelry. You may find an old beaded necklace or bracelet that you no longer wear and would be perfect to recycle into an ornament.

YOU WILL NEED:

Straightedge ruler

Wire cutters

24-gauge wire in silver

8 crystal seed beads

Needle-nose pliers

2 bead caps in silver

Four 7 mm beads, 2 in sky blue
    and 2 in pearl

Three 10 mm beads, 2 in sky blue
    and 1 in pearl

Two 15 mm beads, 1 in sky blue
    and 1 in pearl

One 10 mm crystal bead

1. Using ruler and wire cutters, measure and cut a 12-inch piece of wire.

2. To string bottom bead, insert one end of wire into a crystal seed bead. Slide bead 1 inch up wire. Take same end of wire and bring it up and around bead, inserting it into same hole. Pull ends taut to trap bead in loop. Using wire cutters, trim bottom wire to $^3/_8$ inch. Use needle-nose pliers to bend into loop.

3. To string remaining beads, beginning at opposite end of wire, slide on a bead cap. Add a sky blue 7 mm bead, a crystal seed bead, and then a pearl 7 mm bead followed by a crystal seed bead. Add remaining sky blue and pearl 7 mm beads, placing a seed bead after each one.

4. Add a sky blue 10 mm bead followed by a crystal seed bead. Add a pearl 10 mm bead and a crystal seed bead in the same fashion as in step 3. End with a sky blue 10 mm bead and another seed bead.

5. Slide on the pearl 15 mm bead, the 10 mm crystal bead, and then the sky blue 15 mm bead. Finish with remaining bead cap at top.

6. Form remaining wire into loop and twist at top of end cap. Use wire cutters to trim any excess wire.

Silver Snowball

Bring the outdoors inside by making this cool, icy ornament. The "snow" on the glass ball appears to have melted in the sunshine and refrozen in the night, creating ice crystals that shimmer in the light.

YOU WILL NEED:

Kraft paper

3-inch-diameter clear glass ball with
    removable metal cap

6-inch-square Styrofoam block

Drinking straw

Spray paint in metallic silver

High-tack white glue

Plastic winter snow

Small round beads in silver

Note: Always work in a well-ventilated
    area when using spray paint.

1. Cover clean, flat work surface with kraft paper. Remove cap from glass ball and set aside.

2. To facilitate painting, place Styrofoam block on work surface and stick straw in center. Insert cap end of glass ball on straw. Coat surface of ball with spray paint. Let dry completely. Lift glass ball off straw.

3. Holding ball upright, cover U-shaped areas with glue, beginning at top of ball and coming down sides. Make U-shapes shorter than desired end result, because high-tack glue will elongate slightly. Sprinkle plastic snow and then silver beads onto glued areas. Let dry completely.

4. Replace cap on ball.

Snowy Pinecone

This pinecone painted in icy winter colors with sparkling glitter accents is perfect for hanging on a Christmas tree. It also makes a wonderful favor for your holiday guests. Create one for each place setting at your holiday table, then insert a slip of paper with the guest's name in the leaves of the pinecone. At the end of the evening, everyone will have new ornaments to bring home and hang on their own trees.

YOU WILL NEED:

Kraft paper

Small pinecone

Rubber gloves

Spray primer in white

Gloss spray paint in mint blue or green

Spray adhesive

Plastic winter snow

Fine glitter in warm highlight

$^1/_3$ yard of thin silver twisted cording

Scissors

Note: Always work in a well-ventilated area when using spray paint.

1. Cover clean, flat work surface with kraft paper. Place pinecone on paper.

2. Put on rubber gloves. Apply thin coat of spray primer to pinecone. Let dry completely. Apply one or two more coats of primer, as necessary. Let dry completely.

3. Apply thin coat of spray paint to pinecone. Let dry completely. Apply one to two more coats of paint, as necessary. Let dry completely.

4. Apply fine mist of spray adhesive to painted pinecone. Wait 5 minutes or until cone is tacky.

5. Lightly sprinkle plastic snow on pinecone until it sticks and desired effect is achieved. Take a pinch of glitter and sprinkle over pinecone. Let dry completely.

6. Make loop with silver cording and tie in double knot around top prong of pinecone. Trim ends, if necessary, with scissors.

Frosted-Glass Ball

Re-create the beautiful look of frosted windowpanes on a cold winter morning. A plain glass ball is transformed in minutes into a frosted work of art simply by using press type and etching cream.

YOU WILL NEED:

Kraft paper

3-inch-diameter clear glass ball with
    removable metal cap

Glass cleaner

Paper towels

Self-adhesive press-type letters

6-inch-square Styrofoam block

Drinking straw

Rubber gloves

Etching cream

Sponge brush

Dish towel

Note: Follow manufacturer's directions
    carefully when using etching cream.
    Always wear rubber gloves and do not
    allow cream to come in contact with
    skin, eyes, or mucous membranes.

1. Cover clean, flat work surface with kraft paper. Remove cap from glass ball and set aside.

2. Using glass cleaner and paper towels, remove all grease and fingerprints from glass ball.

3. Peel press-type letters from sheet, one at a time, to spell NOEL, or as desired. Place on glass ball and press down gently. Smooth out any wrinkles and bubbles.

4. To facilitate etching, place Styrofoam block on work surface and stick straw in center. Insert cap end of glass ball on straw.

5. Put on rubber gloves. Following manufacturer's directions, pat (do not brush) thick coat of etching cream on glass ball using sponge brush. (Note: Brushing across glass will increase chances of cream seeping under press type and blurring lines.) Let sit 5 minutes.

6. Still wearing gloves, lift glass ball off straw and place under running water. Rinse away all cream, rubbing glass ball with gloved hands if necessary.

7 Pat glass ball dry with dish towel. Remove letters and replace metal end cap.

Organandy Sleeve for Mini-Lights

Mini-lights emit a soft glow when slipped into a sleeve of gossamer-thin organdy, creating a romantic holiday atmosphere. Be sure to read the caution note below before using your sleeve.

YOU WILL NEED:

Strand of mini-lights in white

3-inch-wide cotton organdy tube ribbon in white or ice blue, twice length of light strand

Two 4-inch lengths monofilament

Scissors

$1/2$ yard of 1-inch-wide satin ribbon in white

Substitute for tube ribbon: Fold 6-inch-wide organdy ribbon in half lengthwise. Machine-stitch $1/8$ inch from edge. Turn ribbon inside out.

CAUTION: Choose an organdy ribbon that is cotton and not one with metallic fibers. Never use mini-lights that have broken or cracked sockets, are frayed, are missing bulbs, or have loose or exposed wires. Doing so may cause electric shock or start a fire. Do not leave covered lights on unattended.

1. Feed one end of mini-lights into tube ribbon. When lights reach opposite end of ribbon, use one length monofilament to tie ribbon in place. Be sure to leave plug exposed.

2. Push ribbon down string of mini-lights until all lights are covered. Leave opposite plug exposed and secure ribbon with remaining length monofilament.

3. Smooth out ribbon, evenly distributing gathers.

4. Using scissors, cut satin ribbon in half. Tie bows over monofilament at each end.

Crystal Ball with Plumage

The grace of a pure white feather is accentuated when it is showcased in an ice-clear glass ball and dusted with fine glitter. Its simple elegance is enhanced when placed on a lush branch of evergreen. Try combining feathers in fuchsia or turquoise with coordinating colors of glitter for a festive variation.

3-inch-diameter clear glass ball with removable metal cap

White feather, 3 to 4 inches long

Tweezers

Micro glitter in gold or silver to match metal cap (optional)

Piece of scrap paper (optional)

$1/2$ yard silver-trimmed white organdy ribbon, $1/2$ inch wide

Scissors

1. Remove cap from glass ball and set aside.

2. Insert feather into neck of glass ball, fluffy end first, until entire feather is inside ball, leaving quill end resting in neck. Use tweezers, if necessary, to position feather. If desired, sprinkle a pinch of micro glitter on scrap paper; fold paper and funnel glitter into neck of ball.

3. Replace cap.

4. Run ribbon through hook in cap, pulling cording to midpoint. Tie knot at top to make loop. Trim ends with scissors.

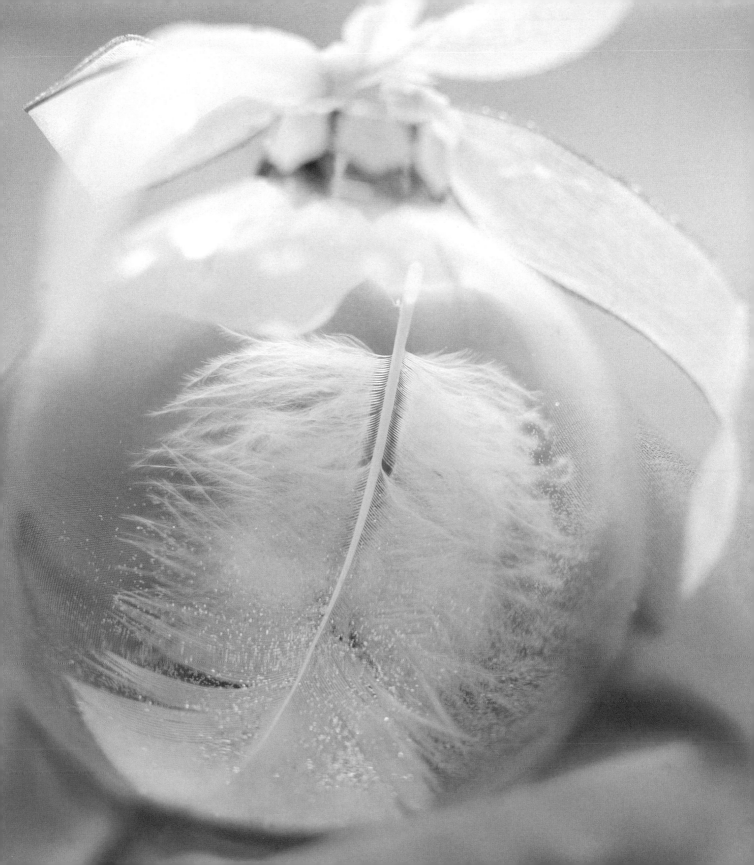

winter gardens

2

Beaded Pears

Turn a simple green Styrofoam pear into a sparkling ornament by encrusting it with decorative glass beads called Teenie Weenie Beadies™. These small, clear beads make the colors of the pear shine in the light. Make one to hang on your tree, or make several and feature them in a bowl as a beautiful centerpiece at your holiday celebration.

YOU WILL NEED:

Kraft paper

Plastic-covered Styrofoam pear with

   stem, 2 inches high, in green, yellow,

   or as desired

6-inch-square Styrofoam block

Straightedge ruler (optional)

Wire cutters (optional)

24-gauge wire (optional)

Mod Podge™

Sponge brush

2 ounces clear Teenie Weenie Beadies™

Small bowl

Tweezers

Hot-glue gun and glue sticks

Silk leaf in green

1. Cover clean, flat work surface with kraft paper. Stick stem of pear into Styrofoam block and place on work surface. If stem is too short, use ruler and wire cutters to measure and cut a 6-inch length of wire. Wrap wire around stem two or three times, then insert free end of wire in block.

2. Lightly coat body of pear with Mod Podge using sponge brush. Rotate Styrofoam block to apply glue evenly on all sides.

3. Pour Teenie Weenie Beadies into small bowl. Using tweezers, grasp stem of pear and remove from Styrofoam block. Gently roll pear in beads until completely covered, leaving stem bare. Replace stem in block. Let dry completely.

4. Remove pear from Styrofoam block. Using hot-glue gun, apply small dab of glue to stem of pear and attach leaf. Hold leaf in place for a few seconds until secure.

Miniature Pepper Berry Wreath

The understated beauty of clusters of red berries accented with a snowy white ribbon makes this sweet little wreath a timeless addition to your collection of treasured keepsake ornaments. Holly or canella berries may be substituted for the pepper berries.

YOU WILL NEED:

Floral tape in green

3-inch-diameter Styrofoam ring

Pepper berry branches

1/2-inch floral pins

Hot-glue gun and glue sticks

1/3 yard of 5/8-inch-wide wire-edged
   organdy ribbon in white

Scissors

Ornament hook

1. Wrap floral tape around entire surface area of ring. Lay flat on clean work surface, wrong-side up.

2. Break branches into small lengths and attach to Styrofoam ring, using floral pins. Cover pins with berries, attaching them with glue gun. Repeat until ring and pins are covered.

3. Gently turn wreath over and repeat step 2. Berries are delicate; do not press down on wreath. If berries come loose, reattach using glue gun.

4. Tie organdy ribbon to a floral pin, making knot at midpoint of ribbon. Tie a bow and trim edges with scissors if necessary. Push floral pin with bow into top of wreath to secure.

5. Push hook into Styrofoam ring at top of wreath near bow. Use floral pin to secure if necessary. Arrange bow and berries to cover insertion site of hook.

Citrus Slices

One of the favorite traditions in my family was to decorate the Christmas tree with slices of candied fruit, then eat them all on Christmas morning before breakfast was served. You can create sparkling fruit slices in vibrant colors that will last for years, using Styrofoam, glue, and glitter. These ornaments also make attractive accents for gift packages.

Cookie sheet

Kitchen aluminum foil

3-inch-diameter juice glass or

disposable plastic lid

Styrofoam sheet, $\frac{1}{4}$ inch thick

Pencil

Straightedge ruler

Scissors

Tweezers

#4 natural-bristle paintbrush

High-tack white glue

Fine glitter in pastel pink, lemon

yellow, and warm highlight

Citrus section pattern (page 103)

Wooden skewer

Two $\frac{1}{2}$-yard lengths of $\frac{1}{8}$-inch-wide

ribbon, 1 in pastel pink and

1 in lemon yellow

Four 3 mm beads, 2 in pastel pink

and 2 in lemon yellow

1. Cover cookie sheet with aluminum foil. Set aside.

2. Place glass or lid on Styrofoam sheet and trace around outer edge with pencil. Using straightedge ruler, mark two opposite points along circumference and draw line through center of circle, dividing it in two equal halves.

3. Cut out circle using scissors. Cut along center line to create two half circles. Set one aside.

4. While holding half circle with tweezers, use paintbrush to spread glue evenly over one side and outside edges. Sprinkle glued areas with pink glitter. Lay on cookie sheet and sprinkle glitter on area where tweezers were. Let dry completely.

5. Turn half circle over on cookie sheet. Use points of tweezers to hold half circle down and apply glue with paintbrush. Sprinkle glued area with pink glitter. Let dry completely.

6. To add citrus sections, use pattern on page 103 as a guide to apply thin lines of glue, using nozzle of glue bottle and even pressure on one side of half circle. Sprinkle warm highlight glitter over glued lines. Let dry completely. Gently shake off extra glitter. Repeat on opposite side.

7. Use skewer to poke hole in top center area of straight edge of glittered slice. Pull pink ribbon through hole until midpoint. Slide one pink bead on each end of ribbon and let beads slide down ribbon. Make a knot $\frac{1}{4}$ inch from each end. Slide beads up ribbon against knots and tie ends together, knotting them below beads.

8. Repeat steps 4 through 7 using yellow glitter, ribbon, and beads for second half circle.

Crystal Butterflies for Mini-Lights

These mesh butterflies, coated in crystal glitter, sparkle and shine when placed on a strand of mini-lights. Each bulb becomes the body of the butterfly when it is positioned between the wings. The butterflies are simple so you can make enough to decorate an entire strand of lights. If you're pressed for time, create just a few of these elegant ornaments, and string fine silver cord through the top of each to make a loop for hanging. Be sure to read the caution note before using your butterflies.

Kraft paper

Plastic mesh

Spray paint in silver

Pencil

Butterfly pattern (page 103)

Tracing paper

Scissors

Work gloves

Spray adhesive

Coarse glass glitter in clear crystal

High-tack white glue

Fine glitter in silver or warm highlight

Monofilament

Strand of mini-lights in white

Note: Always work in well-ventilated area when using spray paint and spray adhesive.

CAUTION: Place butterflies against plastic-covered bulb casing or on plastic-covered wires only, never on bulb. Never use mini-lights that have broken or cracked sockets, are frayed, are missing bulbs, or have loose or exposed wires. Doing so may cause electric shock or start a fire. Do not leave covered lights on unattended.

1. Cover clean, flat work surface with kraft paper. Lay sheet of mesh flat on work surface. Apply light coat of spray paint to mesh and let dry completely. Repeat on opposite side.

2. Using pencil, trace butterfly pattern on page 103 onto tracing paper. Cut out pattern and lay flat on mesh. Trace around template with pencil.

3. Put on work gloves and cut out butterfly shape using scissors.

4. Place mesh butterfly on kraft paper and apply light coat of spray adhesive. Wait 5 minutes or until mesh is tacky. Both sides tend to get sticky at same time because mesh lets glue seep through. If necessary, turn butterfly over and apply light coat of spray adhesive.

5. Sprinkle glass glitter over both sides of butterfly until covered or desired effect is achieved. Let dry completely.

6. Run line of glue along outside edge of wings as indicated in pattern, using nozzle of glue bottle. Sprinkle on fine glitter. Shake off excess and let dry completely. Repeat on opposite side. Fold butterfly in half lengthwise. Open butterfly; fold will remain in mesh.

7. Cut a 6-inch length of monofilament. Working from back of butterfly, thread monofilament through mesh in center, slightly right of fold. Bring end through mesh slightly left of fold. Pull monofilament to midpoint. Place back of butterfly flush against plastic-covered casing below mini-light bulb so entire bulb appears above and between top of wings. Tie knot in mono-filament to secure butterfly to bulb casing.

8. Repeat steps 1 through 7 to make additional butterflies.

Ribbon and Roses

Accent your tree with a streamer of shiny satin that cascades from branch to branch. The pink ribbon is draped in one continuous length around the tree and is held in place by painted clips made from ordinary clothespins embellished with silk roses.

YOU WILL NEED:

Kraft paper

Clothespins

Spray paint in pink

Silk roses in pink

Hot-glue gun and glue sticks

⅝-inch-wide ribbon in coordinating color

Scissors

Note: Always work in a well-ventilated area when using spray paint.

1. Cover clean, flat work surface with kraft paper. Place clothespin on paper.

2. Apply light coat of spray paint to clothespin. Let dry completely. Apply second coat, as necessary. Turn clothespin over and repeat on second side.

3. Place clothespin on work surface, hinge facing up. Position and glue rose to center using glue gun, concealing top two V-shaped prongs with rose.

4. Repeat steps 2 and 3 to make desired number of rose clips.

5. Beginning at top of Christmas tree, clip one rose onto branch. Place end of ribbon in clip, hiding end. Drape ribbon and clip on tree with second rose. Continue draping the ribbon from rose to rose, clipping it in place and working around tree and creating garland. Trim end of ribbon with scissors. Hide end with rose clip.

Gilded Apple

Add majesty to a plain plastic-coated Styrofoam apple with elegant gold accents. Dipping fruit into paint that floats on water creates a beautiful webbed effect.

YOU WILL NEED:

Kraft paper

Aluminum roasting pan

Water

Spray paint in metallic gold

Plastic-coated Styrofoam apple with
   stem in red or golden yellow

$1/4$ yard of thin gold twisted
   cording (optional)

Scissors

Note: Always work in a well-ventilated
   area when using spray paint.

1. Cover clean, flat work surface with kraft paper. Fill aluminum roasting pan with water and set up on separate work surface.

2. Spray small amount of paint onto surface of water.

3. Touch surface of apple onto surface of water. Paint will adhere to apple in webbed or speckled pattern. Set aside on kraft paper to dry completely.

4. Repeat step 3, adding more paint if necessary, until surface of apple is covered as desired.

5. To make a loop for hanging, loop gold cording and tie in double knot at base of apple stem. Trim with scissors if necessary.

Jingle-Bell Grape Cluster

Small jingle bells, grouped together and accented with gold leaves, create a musical tree decoration. It can also be hung on a doorknob to offer a sonorous greeting to guests.

YOU WILL NEED:

Straightedge ruler

Wire cutters

30-gauge beading wire in gold

Fifteen 16 mm jingle bells in gold

Small silk grape leaves

Paint pen in gold

$1/4$ yard of $5/8$-inch-wide satin
   ribbon in gold

Scissors

Hot-glue gun and glue sticks

1. Using straightedge ruler and wire cutters, measure and cut a 12-inch length of beading wire.

2. Thread one end of wire through top loop on one bell and twist to secure. Continue adding bells to wire, sliding them to bottom (see diagram a).

3. To create grape cluster, swing bells into different positions around wire (see diagram b). Bunch a few bells at bottom and majority of them at top. When desired shape is achieved, wrap remaining wire around individual bells to secure, finishing with wire at top. Make a loop and twist to secure. Trim away excess wire with wire cutters. Set cluster aside.

4. Coat grape leaves with gold paint, using paint pen.

5. Tie organdy ribbon in small bow. Trim ends with scissors if necessary.

6. Attach leaves and bow to top of grape cluster using glue gun.

a   b

Glitter Dragonfly

This sassy little bug brightens up any tree or gift package. Lime green glitter applied to a strip of Styrofoam forms the body; matching beads strung on wire form the wings. It is that easy! Make a whole gang of dragonflies in vivid colors like pink, orange, and yellow.

YOU WILL NEED:

Straightedge ruler

Pencil

1/4-inch-thick Styrofoam sheet

Scissors

#4 natural-bristle paintbrush

High-tack white glue

Micro glitter in lime green

Wire cutters

24-gauge wire

Masking tape

Two-hundred-fifty 2 mm
    beads in lime green

Needle-nose pliers

Thread in lime green

Hand-sewing needle

1. Using ruler and pencil, measure and mark a 3-inch-by-$^3/_8$-inch strip on Styrofoam. Cut out with scissors, rounding ends.

2. Using paintbrush, apply thin coat of white glue to Styrofoam. Sprinkle glitter over glued area. Shake off extra. Set aside to dry completely before repeating on opposite side.

3. Using wire cutters, cut four lengths of wire, each 7 inches long. Set three lengths aside.

4. To prevent beads from slipping off wire, cover bottom inch of one end with piece of masking tape. String beads on wire stopping 1 inch from end. Bend beaded wire into a narrow, wing-shaped loop (as pictured) and twist wire ends at base once. Repeat to make three more wings.

5. Remove tape from two wings and twist ends together to form pair of wings. Using wire cutters, trim ends to slightly longer than $^1/_8$ inch. Repeat to make second pair of wings.

6. Apply dab of glue on one side of Styrofoam $^1/_2$ inch from top. Pierce wire ends of one pair of wings through glue and into styrofoam. Set aside to dry completely before repeating on opposite side.

7. Using wire cutters, cut two lengths of wire, each 3 inches long. Set one length aside.

8. Using pliers, crimp wire end by folding just the tip over to prevent beads from slipping off wire. Curl end of wire length into a spiral (to make antennae as pictured). String beads on wire, sliding beads around the spiral. Stop beading 1 inch from end. Place piece of tape on end. Repeat with second wire length.

9. Remove tape from two antennae and twist ends together to form a V shape with the spirals pointing away from each other. Using wire cutters, trim ends to slightly longer than $\frac{1}{8}$ inch.

10. Apply dab of glue at the top of styrofoam body. Pierce wire ends of antennae through glue and into Styrofoam. Lay flat on work surface to dry completely.

11. Thread needle and pierce sides of Styrofoam $\frac{1}{4}$ inch from top, pulling thread to midpoint. Trim thread and tie double knot at top to make loop.

celestial skies

3

Shooting Star

A star streaks through the night sky leaving a trail of light behind it. A tinsel stem (also known as a pipe cleaner) in the shape of a star creates a similar sparkling effect with streams of golden beads that appear suspended in midair.

YOU WILL NEED:

Straightedge ruler

12-inch tinsel stem in gold

Pencil

24-gauge wire in gold

Wire cutters

Seventy-five 2 mm beads in gold

One 3 mm bead in gold

1. Using straightedge ruler, measure 1⅛ inches from end of tinsel stem. Bend tinsel stem, bringing short length parallel to stem. Continue bending stem like an accordion, using short length as guide. There will be ½ inch left at end.

2. Holding ends, stretch out stem. Find center bend and use as top point of star. Use extra ½ inch to overlap open end and twist to secure. Set aside.

3. Using straightedge ruler and pencil, measure and mark five lengths of wire, each 9 inches long. Cut with wire cutters. Set four pieces aside.

4. Insert end of one length of wire into 2 mm bead. Slide bead 1 inch down wire. Bring long end of wire around bead and insert in hole. Pull ends taut, trapping bead in loop (see diagram 1).

5. Insert long end of wire into second 2 mm bead. Slide bead down wire ½ inch above first bead. Bring long end of wire around second bead and insert into hole. Holding bead at ½ inch mark, pull wire taut, trapping bead in loop. Continue adding beads in the same manner, leaving ½ inch between each one, stopping 1 inch from end.

6. Repeat steps 4 and 5 to string beads on remaining four pieces of wire.

7. Using diagram 2a as a guide, twist end of one length of beaded wire around outside point of star. Arc wire and twist other end

1

2 a   2 b   2 c

around opposite inside point. Attach and arc remaining lengths of beaded wires in same way.

8. Using wire cutters, cut 6-inch length of wire. Gather beaded wires at top point of arc and insert 6-inch length underneath loops (see diagram 2b). Pull until midpoint is reached, bring ends up, gently pull taught, and twist entire length to secure. Straighten and align beaded wires.

9. At top of twisted wire, slide on 3 mm bead, followed by two 2 mm beads. Open remaining twisted ends to create loop (see diagram 2c).

Sunburst Christmas Cracker

Bring a wonderful British tradition to your holiday table. Tubes filled with candy, charms, or little toys are wrapped in decorative paper. A simple strip inside the tube snaps like a firecracker when its ends are pulled (see Note). As tradition goes, one "cracker" is put at every place setting. Guests cross their arms and hold one end of the crackers also held by the adjacent guests. Everyone simultaneously pulls the snaps to reveal their holiday surprise.

YOU WILL NEED:

Bathroom tissue tube

Confetti

Wrapped hard candy

Straightedge ruler

Pencil

Gift wrap in sunburst or star pattern

Scissors

11-inch-long snap

Rubber cement

$1/4$-inch ribbon in coordinating color

Tinsel (optional)

Note: Snaps are 11-inch paper strips that
   have a bit of gunpowder in the middle
   and can be mail-ordered (page 102).
   They are rolled up within the gift wrap
   and tube with the ends sticking out.
   The project can also be made without
   the snap if desired. Simply tear the
   ends open to reveal the gifts inside.

1. Fill tube with confetti and candy. Set aside.

2. Using straightedge ruler and pencil, measure and mark a 12-inch-by-6-inch rectangle on gift wrap. Cut out with scissors.

3. Position gift wrap horizontally on work surface, wrong-side up. Measure and mark two points on bottom edge, each $3^3/4$ inches in from right and left edges. Measure and mark two points on top edge, also $3^3/4$ inches in from right and left edges.

4. Center tube horizontally on gift wrap between two marked points and 2 inches from bottom edge. Center and lay snap 1 inch above and parallel to tube on gift wrap.

5. Apply line of rubber cement along bottom edge between marked points. Roll paper up and onto tube, pressing to adhere. Apply second line of rubber cement along top edge between marked points. Bring top edge of paper down, wrapping it snugly around tube and trapping snap inside. Press down to adhere.

6. Measure, mark, and cut two lengths of ribbon 20 inches long.

7. Wrap 1 length of ribbon around gift wrap at right end of tube. While keeping tube from shifting, tie a knot at midpoint of ribbons and cinch tightly; then tie a bow. Repeat on left end. If desired, tie tinsel around each end.

Blue Moon

The silhouette of a crescent moon is highlighted when placed against a glittering field of sky made from heavy-gauge aluminum foil. Easy to work with, this high-sheen foil can be embossed with a pencil eraser and cut with scissors. Make the moon decoration in any phase you like.

YOU WILL NEED:

Kraft paper

Straightedge ruler

Pencil with blunt tip and eraser

36-gauge tooling foil

Scissors

Thick magazine

Moon pattern (page 103)

Tracing paper

Masking tape

4-inch-diameter disposable plastic lid

Awl

Air-dry surface conditioner for glass

Soft-bristle paintbrush

Air-dry transparent glass paint in
    royal blue

High-tack white glue

Micro glitter in silver

Spray acrylic sealer

$1/3$ yard of $5/8$-inch-wide satin
    ribbon in silver

Note: Always work in well-ventilated area
    when using glass paint and acrylic spray.

1. Cover clean, flat work surface with kraft paper.

2. Using straightedge ruler and pencil, measure and mark a 6-inch square on tooling foil. Cut out with scissors.

3. Place foil on magazine. Smooth flat with hands.

4. Using pencil, trace moon pattern on page 103 onto tracing paper.

5. Place pattern on foil right-side up. Secure with masking tape. Using tip of pencil, run light pressure over lines of pattern, slightly indenting foil. Lift tracing paper from foil. Trace over indentations on foil with a heavier hand, using tip of pencil. To get a clean outer circle, use plastic lid.

6. Turn foil over. Rub crescent moon area only with pencil eraser, using circular motion. This creates a raised surface on opposite side. Punch small hole at top using awl. Turn foil to right side and cut out full moon using scissors.

7. Apply light coat of surface conditioner to non-raised area only, using clean, dry paintbrush. Let conditioner dry completely. Wash paintbrush with soap and water. Let brush dry completely.

8. Apply light coat of glass paint to non-raised area using paintbrush. Let paint dry completely. Wash brush and let dry completely. Brush second light coat on crescent. Let paint dry completely.

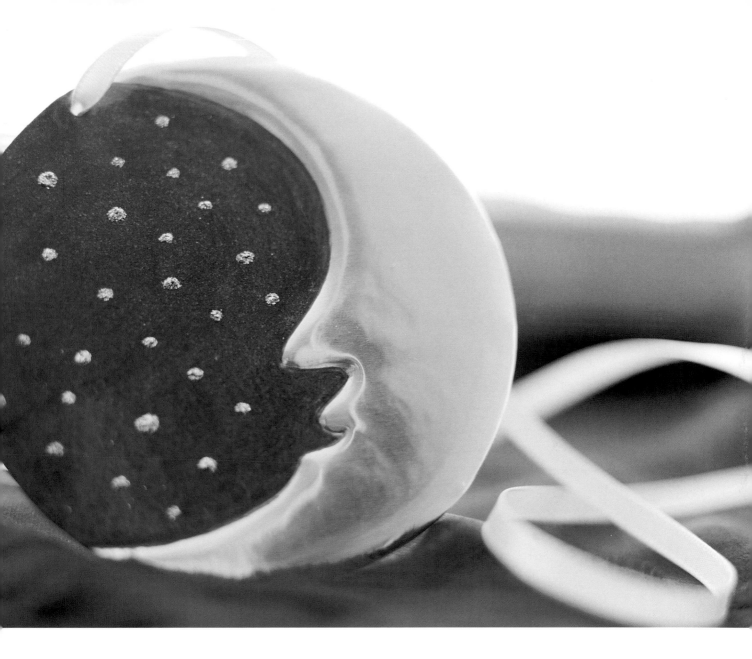

9. To create stars, apply dots of glue to painted foil area using nozzle of glue bottle. Sprinkle glitter over glued area. Let dry completely. Shake off excess glitter.

10. Apply thin coat of acrylic sealer to moon.

11. Run ribbon through hole, pulling it to midpoint, and tie ends in double knot to form loop.

Glitter Galaxy

Applying glitter is a great way to revive ordinary colored ball ornaments you already own. All you need is glue, along with glitter, and a little imagination to create any design you like. You can also personalize an ornament by writing someone's name on the side. Use the nozzle of the glue bottle to write the name, then apply glitter. Date the other side using the same method, and you've created a holiday keepsake.

YOU WILL NEED:

Cookie sheet

Kitchen aluminum foil

3-inch-diameter pink glass ball ornament with removable metal cap

6-inch-square Styrofoam block

Drinking straw

High-tack white glue

Micro glitter in coordinating color

1. Cover cookie sheet with aluminum foil. Remove cap from glass ball and set aside.

2. To facilitate decorating, place Styrofoam block on cookie sheet and stick straw in center. Insert cap end of glass ball on straw.

3. Make swirl design or other desired design on surface of ball with nozzle of glue bottle.

4. Sprinkle glitter over glued areas. Let dry completely. Shake off excess glitter. Replace cap.

Starlight Shades for Mini-Lights

Add starry constellations to mini-lights. Parchment punched with star-shaped holes is wrapped around a lid from a film canister to make a shade. When the shades are placed on the lights, the pattern glows like stars in the winter sky. Be sure to read the caution note below before using your shades.

YOU WILL NEED:

Film canister lids in white

Awl

X-Acto knife

Straightedge ruler

Pencil

Vellum in white

Scissors

Star hole punch

High-tack white glue

Strand of mini-lights in white

CAUTION: Film canister lid should sit at base of plastic-covered bulb casing. Never use mini-lights that have broken or cracked sockets, are frayed, are missing bulbs, or have loose or exposed wires. Doing so may cause electric shock or start a fire. Do not leave covered lights on unattended.

1. Separate lids from film canisters. If desired, save canisters for another project; they will not be used.

2. Poke hole in center of one lid with awl. Using hole as guide, very carefully use X-Acto knife to create an "X" in center of lid. Set aside.

3. Using straightedge ruler and pencil, measure and mark a 4-inch-by-$\frac{1}{2}$-inch rectangle on vellum. Cut out with scissors.

4. Lay vellum in horizontal position on clean, flat work surface. Use hole punch to cut stars in random pattern.

5. Apply scant dabs of glue around outside edge of lid. Position and press bottom edge of vellum to lid rim. Where edges meet, apply scant dabs of glue to secure.

6. Carefully push mini-light up through hole in bottom of lid. Position base of lid at base of plastic-covered bulb casing.

7. Repeat steps 1 through 6 for additional shades.

Night Sky

The secret behind this quick-and-easy ornament is the Ultimate Bond™ double-stick tape that comes in precut star shapes. One side sticks to the ornament, and the other side holds glitter. Scatter your stars randomly or create a constellation.

YOU WILL NEED:

Kraft paper

Ultimate Bond™ tape in stars

3-inch-diameter glass ball in blue

Fine glitter in silver

Soft-bristle paintbrush

1. Cover clean, flat work surface with kraft paper.

2. Remove one star sticker from white paper backing of Ultimate Bond™ tape. Do not remove protective pink top sheet. Press star onto glass ball in desired position. Repeat with remaining stars, positioning them randomly over entire ball.

3. Remove protective pink top sheets from stars to reveal second sticky side.

4. Sprinkle glitter over stars. Using paintbrush, gently sweep away excess glitter.

Silvery Moon

Wrap shimmering silver bullion over a wire base to create elegant balls that will add beauty and charm to any tree or mantel. You may even want to place them in a large crystal vase as a centerpiece for your holiday table. Nestle them near the lights on your tree for added sparkle.

YOU WILL NEED:

Wire cutters

16-gauge armature wire

1$\frac{1}{2}$-inch-diameter Styrofoam ball

Scissors

Silver bullion

1. Using wire cutters, cut 8-inch length of armature wire.

2. Wrap wire vertically around Styrofoam ball. After one full wrap, bend wire slightly and again wrap around ball but in new position. Continue wrapping wire, changing position with each full wrap, stopping 2 inches from end.

3. Slide wires to create opening and slip ball out. Reshape globe.

4. Using scissors, cut 6-inch length of silver bullion and wrap around globe horizontally, stretching bullion slightly. Tuck end into globe. Continue cutting lengths of bullion and wrapping them around globe until it is covered.

5. Repeat steps 1 through 4 for additional moons.

favorite things

Monogrammed Velvet Pouch

The lush, deep-sapphire color of this elegant fabric is highlighted by its intrinsic sheen. Pressing down the nap of the velvet with a wooden block creates the embossed monogram. The pouch is a personal way to package any small gift or holiday confections.

YOU WILL NEED:

Iron

Straightedge ruler

Pencil

Rayon velvet in blue

Scissors

Wooden block letter or rubber
   stamp in monogram, as desired

Cookie sheet

Spray starch

Straight pins

Thread in blue

Sewing machine

$1/2$ yard of $1/4$-inch-wide velvet ribbon
   in coordinating color

1. Remove all water from iron. Turn iron on to hottest setting.

2. Using straightedge ruler and pencil, measure and mark two rectangles of velvet, each 8 inches by 7 inches. Press velvet on wrong side with iron to remove any wrinkles in fabric. Cut out with scissors. Set aside.

3. Place wooden block, letter side up, on cookie sheet. Center one piece of velvet, wrong-side up, over monogram. Lightly spray velvet with starch.

4. Press velvet with iron, holding iron down for 10 seconds. Do not slide iron across fabric as it may blur monogram.

5. Lay velvet rectangles side by side, vertically and wrong-sides up, on clean, flat work surface. At top edges, measure, fold, and stitch a 1-inch hem.

6. Turn one velvet rectangle right-side up. Position second rectangle of velvet over first, right-sides together. Align raw edges and hems at top. Pin sides and bottom, leaving hemmed top open.

7. Using thread, machine-stitch $1/2$-inch seam around outside raw edges.

8. Clip corners, remove pins, and trim loose threads. Turn to right side.

9. Fill pouch with candy or a gift and tie closed with ribbon.

Framed Holiday Scene

Instead of throwing out those Christmas cards you get every year, or tucking them away in a box in the closet, why not recycle them into a masterpiece that you've matted and framed yourself? Choose an appropriate small scene from a Christmas card that would be enhanced by a small wooden plaque that serves as the frame and is embellished with gold leaf. Presanded plaques are easily found in craft stores and have decorative edges to make getting started incredibly easy.

Kraft paper

3$\frac{1}{2}$-inch-by-5-inch presanded

wooden plaque

Tack cloth

Rubber cement

Gold composition leaf

Pencil with eraser

Self-healing mat

Straightedge ruler

Medium-weight patterned paper

in coordinating color

Christmas card

X-Acto knife

Soft-bristle paintbrush

Acrylic sealer

Hammer

2 finishing nails

8 inches of $\frac{1}{4}$-inch-wide

coordinating ribbon

Note: Always work in well-ventilated area

when using gold size and acrylic sealer.

1. Cover clean, flat work surface with kraft paper.

2. Wipe down plaque with tack cloth to remove dust or other particles. Place plaque right-side up on work surface. Apply light coat of rubber cement to front and sides of plaque.

3. Tear off pieces from sheet of gold leaf and place on front and sides of plaque. Tamp down with pencil eraser. When plaque is covered, gently press down and rub gold leaf with fingers. If uncovered areas remain, tear off pieces of gold leaf and reapply.

4. Repeat steps 2 and 3 for opposite side of plaque. Set aside.

5. Working on self-healing mat and using straightedge ruler and pencil, measure and mark a 4-inch-by-2$\frac{1}{4}$-inch rectangle from patterned paper, and a 3$\frac{1}{2}$-inch-by-1$\frac{3}{4}$-inch rectangle from Christmas card. Cut out rectangles with X-Acto knife. Center and glue scene from Christmas card on patterned paper, using rubber cement. Apply rubber cement to back of patterned paper and center and glue onto plaque.

6. Using paintbrush, apply light coat of acrylic sealer to front and sides of plaque. Let dry completely.

7. Hammer finishing nails halfway into back of plaque, $\frac{1}{2}$ inch from top and side edge. Knot ends of ribbon to nails and hammer in nails completely.

Gift-Wrapped Packages

These miniature gifts are delightful when made in coordinating gift wraps and bundled in satin ribbon. Or try combining flocked velvet and glittered and glossy papers in different shades of mint green, accenting them with a bow in icy pink.

YOU WILL NEED:

3 scraps of gift wrap, slightly larger than block sizes

3 balsa wood blocks in graduated sizes, 2 inches by $1/2$ inch, $1^1/2$ inches by $1/2$ inch, 1 inch by $1/2$ inch

Scissors

High-tack white glue

$1/2$ yard of $1/4$-inch-wide satin ribbon in pink

Ornament hook

1. Lay largest scrap of gift wrap on work surface, wrong-side up. Center largest block on gift wrap and trim raw edges with scissors if necessary. Fold long sides of paper around block. Where gift wrap meets, secure with small dab of glue. On short sides, fold in corners, fold sides up, and secure with glue.

2. Repeat step 1 with remaining blocks and gift wrap.

3. Stack wrapped blocks, placing largest on bottom, smallest on top.

4. Center midpoint of ribbon on top package and run down opposite sides of packages and across bottom of largest block. Twist ribbon and bring up adjacent sides of packages. Tie a bow at top and trim ends of ribbon.

5. Attach ornament hook to bow at top of packages.

Cellophane Bows for Mini-Lights

A beautiful way to dress up little white lights is to accent them with colorful cellophane "bows." Use one color for a monochromatic look, or alternate lime green, turquoise, and hot pink to add spice to your holiday tree. If you don't want to do the entire strand, cover every other light and run the lights across your holiday table.

YOU WILL NEED:

Straightedge ruler

Pencil

Cellophane in pink

Scissors

Strand of mini-lights in white

Small rubber band in red

Gold bullion

CAUTION: Wrap rubber bands and gold bullion around cellophane gift bows at base of plastic-covered bulb casing and plastic-coated wires. Cellophane should not touch bulbs. Never use mini-lights that have broken or cracked sockets, that are frayed, are missing bulbs, or have loose or exposed wires. Doing so may cause electric shock or start a fire. Do not leave covered lights on unattended.

1. Using straightedge ruler and pencil, measure and mark a 4-inch-by-4-inch square on cellophane. Cut out with scissors.

2. Hold cellophane in one hand, and with other hand, place one bulb from mini-lights flat on center of cellophane.

3. Gather cellophane from right and left sides toward base of light at plastic-coated bulb casing. Secure at gathered area using rubber band.

4. Cut three pieces of gold bullion, each 1 inch long. Stretch bullion and wrap it over rubber band, gathering and twisting ends at front. Repeat with remaining pieces of bullion. Pull cellophane bow ends away from bulb. Cellophane should not touch bulb.

5. Repeat steps 1 through 4 to make additional bows.

Peppermint Candy Stick

Christmas is the time to indulge in sweets. You can turn a small dowel into a peppermint candy treat by covering it in colorful ribbon stripes. Bundle a trio of these cool confections together with a big bow, add an ornament hook, and hang them on your tree. Or use them as decorations on gift-wrapped packages.

Cookie sheet

Kitchen aluminum foil

Scissors

Four 1-foot lengths of $^1/_4$-inch-wide ribbon, 1 in light pink, 1 in dark pink, 1 in red, and 1 in white

Glue stick

4-inch length of $^5/_8$-inch-wide wooden dowel

Two $^1/_4$-inch sticker dots in red

1. Cover cookie sheet with aluminum foil.

2. Using scissors, cut ribbon lengths in half to form eight 6-inch lengths. Set all aside but one.

3. Lay ribbon length on cookie sheet. Using glue stick, apply thin coat of glue to one side of ribbon, leaving $^1/_4$ inch unglued at one end.

4. Adhere glued end of ribbon to top of dowel. Twist ribbon around dowel, creating a spiral. Leave approximately 1 inch between spirals. Adhere ribbon to bottom of dowel. Snip off excess ribbon. Set dowel aside and allow to dry completely.

5. Repeat steps 3 and 4 with remaining lengths of ribbon, overlapping and alternating colors of ribbon as desired. You may not need all ribbon lengths to completely cover the dowel.

6. Place red sticker dots at top and bottom dowel. If necessary, reinforce with glue.

Miniature Velvet Stocking

Whether large or small, stockings conjure up thoughts of precious gifts and confections spilling out the top, and anticipating that last gift hiding in the toe. Simple cutting and sewing are all that is required to make this ornament for tree or package.

YOU WILL NEED:

Pencil

Stocking and cuff patterns (page 104)

Tracing paper

Scissors

12-inch square of velvet in green

Straight pins

10-inch square of velvet in red

Sewing machine

Matching thread

Small beads or buttons in
   coordinating colors

1. Using pencil, trace stocking and cuff patterns on page 104 on tracing paper. Repeat to create 2 stocking and 2 cuff patterns. Cut out all 4 pattern pieces using scissors.

2. Place green velvet square, wrong-side up, on clean, flat work surface. Lay stocking patterns flat on velvet, one toe facing right, one toe facing left. Secure with pins. Cut out stocking pieces using scissors. Remove pins and pattern from fabric.

3. Place red velvet square, wrong-side up, on clean, flat work surface. Lay cuff patterns flat on velvet. Secure with pins. Cut out cuff pieces using scissors. Remove pins and pattern.

4. Lay one stocking piece of velvet right-side up. Place one cuff piece on top, right-side up, top edges matching. Pin in place and machine-stitch ½ inch from top edge (see diagram a). Using scissors, trim seam to ¼ inch. Open seam, lifting cuff away from stocking. With seam facing down, stocking should be right-side up and cuff wrong-side up (see diagram b).

5. Repeat step 4 with remaining cuff piece and stocking piece.

6. Place stockings right-sides together (cuffs will be wrong-sides together), seams facing out. Pin in place and machine-stitch around the stocking $1/2$ inch from edge (see diagram c). Do not stitch top edges together.

7. Using scissors, trim seam to $1/4$ inch. Turn stocking inside out (cuff will be wrong-side out).

8. Fold $1/2$ inch of cuff down, then fold 2 inches down (see diagrams d and e). Bottom fold of cuff should cover seam between green and red velvet.

9. Hand-stitch small beads or buttons on cuff as desired.

Music-Paper Bell

Old sheet music lends charm to this sweet little bell. The sheets are stacked and cut in the shape of a bell, then sewn together. Ribbon and bead accents finish an ornament to ring in the season.

YOU WILL NEED:

Pencil

Paper bell pattern (page 104)

Tracing paper

Scissors

5 pieces of sheet music

13 inches of 1-inch-wide organdy
   ribbon in coordinating color

Sewing machine

Thread in coordinating color

Paint pen in gold

Two 10 mm wooden beads

High-tack white glue

1. Using pencil, trace bell pattern on page 104 on tracing paper. Cut out with scissors.

2. Fold one piece of sheet music in half vertically. Place bell pattern flush with folded edge and trace around shape with pencil. Cut along traced lines with scissors. Open to reveal whole bell.

3. Repeat step 2 to cut a total of ten bells.

4. Stack bells together, making sure edges are even. Lay ribbon along center fold of top bell in stack, leaving 2 inches at bottom. Machine-stitch through all thicknesses of ribbon and bells along center fold. Trim thread.

5. Using paint pen, paint wooden beads gold. Set aside to dry completely.

6. Slide one bead onto ribbon at bottom of bell. Tie double knot to secure.

7. Slide second bead onto ribbon at top of bell. Insert end of ribbon into top of bead. Tie double knot below bead and at top of bell to secure. Slide bead down to hide knot.

8. Run small line of glue on ribbon along center fold. Press sheets together to help hide ribbon. Fan out sheets to create dimensional bell.

Bottle of Bubbly

Holiday celebrations are full of toasts, good wishes, and bottles of champagne. This crystal-encrusted bottle is made with sculpting clay that you bake in an oven. A painted medicine cup serves as the ice bucket, and crumpled cellophane as the ice. Sprinkle on translucent fine glass glitter for an icy effect.

Kraft paper

Oven-bake polymer clay in pearl green

Champagne bottle pattern (page 104)

Cookie sheet

Kitchen aluminum foil

Oven

Spray paint in metallic silver

Plastic medicine cup

Scissors

30-gauge wire in silver

Straight pin

2 small jewelry jump rings

Cellophane in clear

Foil and label from neck of

   champagne bottle

High-tack white glue

Spray adhesive (optional)

Fine glass glitter in clear crystal (optional)

Note: Always work in well-ventilated area

   when using oven-bake clay, spray paint,

   and spray adhesive.

1. Cover clean, flat work surface with kraft paper.

2. Tear off a 1-inch-by-2-inch rectangle of clay. Using palms, roll into $2^{1}/_{2}$-inch-long log and taper one end. Use bottle pattern on page 104 as a guide and shape clay to achieve bottle shape.

3. Line cookie sheet with aluminum foil. Place clay bottle on cookie sheet. Following clay manufacturer's directions, bake at 275°F for about 30 minutes. Remove from oven and let cool.

4. Apply light coat of silver paint to outside of medicine cup. Let dry completely.

5. Using scissors, cut two pieces of wire, each 2 inches long. Using straight pin, poke two small holes in one side of medicine cup, one on top of the other. Thread wire from inside through one hole, loop wire through ring and thread wire through second hole. Twist wire and trim ends. Repeat on opposite side of cup for second ring.

6. Using scissors, cut a 6-inch square of cellophane and place in bucket, crumpling it until it is entirely in bucket.

7. Using scissors, cut a 1-inch-diameter circle and a 2-inch-by-$^{1}/_{2}$-inch rectangle from champagne foil. Place small amount of glue on circle and bend over top of bottle. Glue rectangle to midsection of bottle. Let dry completely. Place bottle in bucket. Add more cellophane if necessary (optional).

8. If desired, apply light coat of spray adhesive to bottle and bucket. Wait 5 minutes or until tacky. Sprinkle glitter to coat bucket and bottle. Let dry completely.

Silk Candy Box

This simple folded box, evoking the elegance of origami, is perfect for holding candy or small gifts. The simple pattern is mounted on cardboard to make a durable template. Choose light fabric in different colors and patterns, or try using elegant papers and gift wrap instead.

Box pattern (page 105)

YOU WILL NEED:

Pencil

Straightedge ruler

Box pattern (page 105)

Tracing paper

Kraft paper

12-inch square of thin cardboard

Spray adhesive

Self-healing mat

X-Acto knife

12-inch square of cardstock

Fork

12-inch square of patterned silk fabric

Scissors (standard and manicure)

Awl

High-tack white glue

Wire cutters

16-gauge wire in silver

Pliers

Note: Always work in a well-ventilated area when using spray adhesive.

1. Using pencil and straightedge ruler, trace box pattern on page 105 on tracing paper.

2. Cover clean, flat work surface with kraft paper.

3. Place cardboard on kraft paper and apply light coat of spray adhesive. Wait 5 minutes or until cardboard is tacky. Lay pattern, right-side up, on cardboard, and smooth flat with hands, adhering tracing paper and cardboard together. Place on self-healing mat and use X-Acto knife and straightedge ruler to cut out pattern outside bold lines.

4. Lay pattern, right-side up, on cardstock and trace around outside edges with pencil. Lift off pattern. Place cardstock on self-healing mat and cut along outside bold lines using X-Acto knife.

5. Score cardstock along indicated fold lines using straightedge and tines of fork. Place on kraft paper and apply light coat of spray adhesive. Wait 5 minutes or until cardstock is tacky. Lay fabric, right-side up, on cardstock and smooth flat with hands. Turn so cardstock faces up.

6. Fold up sides of box using straightedge as guide, then smooth flat again. (Note: Folding before trimming fabric prevents fabric from being stretched and possibly creating uneven edges.)

7. Trim fabric even with cardstock edges using scissors. Use manicure scissors to negotiate area around closure.

8. Cut slit, as indicated in pattern, using X-Acto knife. Be sure to use new blade to prevent fabric from fraying.

9. Use awl to create holes, as indicated on pattern.

10. Fold container together. Use glue to adhere small tabs A, B, C, and D to inside of box.

11. Using wire cutters, cut a $7^3/_4$-inch length of silver wire. Measure and mark four points from left edge of wire: at $1/_2$ inch, $2^1/_2$ inches, $5^1/_4$ inches, and $7^1/_4$ inches. Using pliers, bend wire up at outside marked points, creating two right angles. Using pliers, bend wire up at two inside marked points, creating two more right angles.

12. Insert ends of wire into holes on sides of box. Use pliars to bend wires flush against inside of box on both sides.

5

miniature toys

Gingerbread House

A light inside this little house streams through the window and also illuminates the rows of candylike beads that cover the miniature domicile. This gingerbread house looks good enough to eat.

YOU WILL NEED:

#1 pencil

Gingerbread pattern (page 106)

Tracing paper

Mat board in pink or yellow

Dry ballpoint pen

Straightedge ruler

Self-healing mat

X-Acto knife

Hot-glue gun and glue sticks

Assorted beads in different shapes
    and in candy colors

High-tack white glue

Plastic winter snow

Kraft paper

Spray adhesive

Fine glass glitter in clear crystal

Strand of mini-lights in white

Note: Always work in a well-ventilated
    area when using spray adhesive.

1. Using pencil, trace house pattern on page 106 on tracing paper.

2. Lay pattern, penciled-side down, on mat board. Use dry ball-point pen and straightedge ruler to trace over lines, pressing down firmly to transfer pencil lines. Lift tracing paper from mat board. A faint penciled pattern will remain on mat board.

3. Place mat board on self-healing mat and cut out house, window, roof, door, base, and hole in base with X-Acto knife. Cut around door, leaving left side attached. Using X-Acto knife and straight edge ruler, score mat board on fold lines as indicated on pattern.

4. To assemble house, bend mat board away from scored lines. Butt adjacent ends together. Run hot glue up inside edge and hold in place to adhere.

5. To add roof, bend mat board away from scored lines. Run hot glue on top edges of house. Position and press roof on house and hold in place to adhere.

6. To add base, run hot glue along bottom edges of house. Center and press base on house and hold in place to adhere.

7. Beginning with roof, apply beads using small dabs of white glue. When roof is covered, glue beads to house.

8. Apply white glue to base around house. Sprinkle on plastic snow. Let dry completely.

9. Cover clean, flat work surface with kraft paper. Set house on paper and apply light coat of spray adhesive. Cover house with glass glitter. Let dry completely.

10. Slip bulb of mini-lights through hole in base of house. Light will shine through cut-out window.

Sugarplum Glass Ball

This glass ball mimics the look of antique frosted-glass ornaments. It combines a number of techniques, which you can use separately if you wish to create a colored ornament, a frosted ornament, or a glittered ornament.

Kraft paper

Newspaper

3-inch-diameter clear glass ball
   with removable metal cap

Glass cleaner

Paper towels

6-inch-square Styrofoam block

Drinking straw

Rubber gloves

Etching cream

Sponge brush

Air-dry transparent glass
   paint in plum

Spray adhesive

Fine glass glitter in clear crystal

Note: Follow manufacturer's directions
   carefully when using etching cream.
   Always wear rubber gloves and do not
   allow cream to come in contact with
   skin, eyes, or mucous membranes.
   Always work in well-ventilated area
   when using spray adhesive.

1. Cover clean, flat work surface with kraft paper. Place a few sheets of newspaper on kraft paper. Remove metal cap from glass ball and set aside.

2. Using glass cleaner and paper towels, remove all grease and fingerprints from glass ball.

3. To facilitate etching, place Styrofoam block on work surface and stick straw in center. Insert cap end of glass ball on straw.

4. Slip on rubber gloves. Following manufacturer's directions, apply etching cream to outside of ball using sponge brush. Let sit 5 minutes. Remove straw and ball from Styrofoam. Rinse off cream under running water. Pat dry with paper towel.

5. Squeeze 1 tablespoon of paint into opening of ball. Turn ball to swirl paint until it coats interior, adding more paint if necessary. Set ball, neck down, on newspaper. Check ornament after 5 minutes to make sure paint has coated ball evenly. Add more paint and continue turning ball if necessary. Let dry completely. If desired, add more coats of paint for a deeper color.

6. Apply very light coat of spray adhesive to outside of ball. Wait 5 minutes or until ball is tacky. Sprinkle light coat of glass glitter on ball. Let dry completely.

7. Replace metal cap.

Vintage Drum

As the song goes, on the twelfth day of Christmas, my true love gave to me twelve drummers drumming. Twelve may be a bit ambitious, but one drum, minus the drummers, makes a charming addition to your tree.

YOU WILL NEED:

Straightedge ruler

Pencil

Bathroom tissue tube

Small hand saw

Scrap of gift wrap in solid color

Scissors

Double-stick tape

Vellum in white

High-tack white glue

$3/4$ yard of $1/8$-inch-wide flat trim in silver

$1/3$ yard of $1/4$-inch-wide flat trim in silver

1. Using straightedge ruler and pencil, measure and mark a $1\frac{1}{4}$-inch piece of tissue tube. Cut with hand saw. Set aside.

2. Measure and mark a $5\frac{1}{4}$-inch-by-$1\frac{1}{4}$-inch rectangle on gift wrap. Cut out with scissors.

3. Lay gift-wrap rectangle horizontally and right-side down on clean, flat work surface. Apply double-stick tape to short ends of rectangle. Place tissue tube on paper. Bring one taped end up and press to adhere. Roll tube along gift wrap, keeping gift wrap flush with tube. Bring up other end of gift wrap, overlapping extra $1/4$ inch of wrap, and press to adhere.

4. Place end of scrap piece of tube on vellum and trace around outside edge with pencil. Trace a second circle. Measure and mark a circle $1/8$ inch outside each original circle. You will now have two $1\frac{3}{4}$-inch-diameter circles. Cut out using scissors. Make small $1/16$-inch cuts every $1/4$ inch around circumference.

5. Run thin line of glue around outside edge of snipped circle. Center circle, glue-side down, over top of drum. Fold and press overhang onto outside of drum to adhere. Repeat for bottom of drum.

6. Beginning at seam of gift wrap, measure and mark $1/2$-inch intervals along bottom edge of drum with pencil ticks. Along top edge of drum, mark $1/4$ inch from seam and then mark at $1/2$-inch intervals with pencil ticks.

7. Measure, mark, and cut a 3-inch piece of narrow trim and set aside.

8. Position and glue one end of remaining narrow trim at marked point of gift-wrap seam on bottom edge of drum. Bring trim up to marked point at top edge and adhere with small dab of glue. Continue positioning and gluing trim around drum at marked intervals. Cut off excess trim where ends meet.

9. Cut wider trim into two equal lengths. Set one aside. Apply small dab of glue at bottom of gift-wrap seam. Position bottom edge of trim on glue, flush with bottom edge of drum, and press to adhere. Continue gluing and pressing trim in place around bottom edge of drum, covering vellum edges. Let dry completely.

10. Make loop with remaining 3-inch piece of narrow trim. Glue ends of loop to gift-wrap seam at top edge of drum. Repeat step 9 to apply remaining wider trim to top edge. Let dry completely.

Rocking Horse

Creating a rocking-horse ornament strung with a shimmering ribbon is as simple as making cookies with store-bought dough. Get your children involved by asking them to cut out the horse, or other shapes, with cookie cutters. Add each child's name with a paint pen on one side and the date on the other to commemorate this year's celebration.

YOU WILL NEED:

Cookie sheet

Kitchen aluminum foil

Rolling pin

Oven-bake polymer clay in pastel color

Cookie cutter in shape of rocking horse

Pencil with eraser

Wooden skewer

Oven

Metallic paint pen in silver

$1/2$ yard of $1/4$-inch-wide ribbon in coordinating color

Note: Always work in well-ventilated area when using oven-bake clay.

1. Line cookie sheet with aluminum foil.

2. With rolling pin, roll out clay $1/4$ inch thick on clean, flat work surface.

3. Press cookie cutter into clay, then lift up. If clay remains in cutter, gently nudge with eraser end of pencil. Place on cookie sheet. Using skewer, poke hole in center of horse, $1/2$ inch from top edge.

4. Following clay manufacturer's directions, bake at 275°F for about 30 minutes. Remove from oven. Let cool.

5. Write name with paint pen on one side of rocking horse. Write date on second side.

6. Thread one end of ribbon through hole and pull to midpoint. Tie ends in double knot to secure.

Baby Block

Baby's first Christmas is a special one. Remember it year after year with this monogrammed block. Created in balsa wood with grooved accents, it recalls the carved version with letters of the alphabet.

YOU WILL NEED:

Kraft paper

$1\frac{1}{2}$-inch-square block of balsa wood

Acrylic paint in yellow

Sponge brush

Acrylic paint in red

Straightedge ruler

Pencil

Balsa wood stick, $\frac{1}{8}$ inch by

   $\frac{1}{8}$ inch by 10 inches long (wooden

   match sticks may also be used)

Hand saw

High-tack white glue

Scissors

1-inch-high stencil letters

Masking tape

Eye hook

$\frac{1}{4}$ yard of fine twisted cording

   in coordinating color

1. Cover clean, flat work surface with kraft paper. Place balsa wood block on paper.

2. Paint top, bottom, right, and left sides yellow using sponge brush. Let dry completely. Paint front and back sides red. Let dry completely.

3. Using straightedge ruler and pencil, measure and mark balsa wood stick into 8 lengths, each $1\frac{1}{4}$ inches. Cut with hand saw. Paint pieces red. Let dry completely.

4. Attach two pieces on left and right edges of top of block with glue. Glue remaining two pieces parallel and between first two pieces. Let dry completely. Turn block over and repeat on bottom with remaining four pieces.

5. Using scissors, cut out desired letter from stencil sheet. Lay block on work surface so one yellow side is facing up. Center stencil on block and secure with masking tape. Load brush with small amount of red paint and pat brush on stencil. Do not use sweeping strokes as lines may blur. Remove tape and lift off stencil. Let dry completely. Repeat on opposite side.

6. To hang, screw eye hook into center of top. Thread cord through hook and pull to midpoint. Tie ends in double knot to form loop.

Red Baron

A purchased plane is enhanced with a shiny coat of red paint and a golden propeller. Balsa airplane kits are readily available in craft stores, and the pieces can be painted and easily assembled in less than ten minutes. Create a squadron in rainbow colors and land them on the boughs of your Christmas tree.

YOU WILL NEED:

Kraft paper

Kit for 4-inch balsa wood
   airplane with propeller

Spray primer in white

Spray paint in red

High-tack white glue

Sponge brush

Micro glitter in gold

Eye hook

$1/4$ yard of $1/4$-inch red organdy ribbon

Note: Always work in well-ventilated
   area when using spray primer and
   spray paint.

1. Cover clean, flat work surface with kraft paper. Place airplane pieces on paper.

2. Apply light coat of spray primer to pieces. Let dry completely. Turn pieces and repeat on second side.

3. Apply light coat of red paint to airplane pieces. Let dry completely. Apply one or two more coats as needed. Turn pieces and repeat on second side.

4. Apply thin coat of glue to propeller using sponge brush. Sprinkle glitter on glued area until covered. Let dry completely.

5. Assemble plane following manufacturer's directions, using glue to secure.

6. To hang, screw eye hook into center of plane. Thread ribbon through hook and pull to midpoint. Tie ends in double knot to form loop.

Harlequin Ball

Golden diamond-shaped panes encase vivid translucent colors on this whimsical ornament. The panes are easy to draw with liquid lead paint and are coated with glitter while still wet. It is impossible to make a mistake: any misstep can be erased with a damp paper towel. Translucent glass paint is then applied to color between the lines.

YOU WILL NEED:

Kraft paper

3-inch-diameter clear glass ball
    with removable metal cap

Glass cleaner

Paper towels

6-inch-square Styrofoam block

Drinking straw

Air-dry surface conditioner for glass

Fine soft-bristle paint brush

Harlequin pattern (page 107)

Air-dry liquid lead paint

Fine glitter in gold

Air-dry transparent glass paint in
    red, blue, yellow, and green

Note: Always work in well-ventilated area
    when using lead and glass paint.

1. Cover clean, flat work surface with kraft paper. Remove metal cap from ball. Set aside.

2. Using glass cleaner and paper towels, remove all grease and fingerprints from glass ball.

3. Place Styrofoam block on work surface and stick straw in center. Insert cap end of glass ball on straw. Following manufacturer's directions, apply light coat of conditioner to glass ball, using paintbrush. Let conditioner dry completely.

4. Remove glass ball from straw and carefully hold ball at bottom. Following pattern for diamond outlines on page 107, use nozzle on bottle of liquid lead paint to apply pattern to area around neck of ball. Continue adding circular rows of diamonds until midpoint of ball. While pattern is still wet, sprinkle with glitter until covered. Shake off excess glitter. Place on work surface to dry completely. Begin at midpoint and add pattern over rest of ball (pattern will narrow as it comes together at bottom). Apply glitter. Place on straw and let dry completely.

5. Following pattern on page 107 for the color diagram, use nozzle on bottle of transparent glass paint (or paintbrush) to lightly color in diamond-shaped panes around neck of ball, alternating

red and blue paint. Then alternate green and yellow. Continue working around neck of ball, keeping in mind colors should be the same moving down verticle rows of ball. (Note: Painting one portion at a time and not using too much paint prevents paint from sliding and dripping.) Place on work surface to dry completely. Repeat for other areas. Replace metal cap.

Glossary of Materials and Tools

acrylic sealer: a gloss varnish applied with a brush to protect projects.

acrylic spray: acrylic sealer in an aerosol form used to varnish and protect projects.

air-dry surface conditioner: a varnish applied with a brush that primes surface of glass, tile, or ceramic so glass paint adheres quickly and easily.

aluminum foil
kitchen: a very thin, silvery sheet of aluminum used to wrap food.
36-gauge tooling: a thick, silvery, lightweight metallic sheet that is very malleable and easily embossed.

armature wire: a highly malleable wire capable of maintaining shape once bent.

awl: a pointed tool for making holes.

balsa wood: an extremely light and easily cut wood.

brush
#4 natural bristle: an all-purpose paintbrush used to apply glue or paint in small areas.
soft bristle: a paintbrush typically made from sable that will apply a smooth coat of paint without leaving bristle lines.
sponge: an inexpensive paintbrush made in various widths. Good for applying glue or paint in broad areas.

bullion: a heavy fringe or lace of twisted gold or silver thread or wire.

cardstock: flat, stiff, heavyweight paper that provides structure and support when laminated to other lightweight papers, gift wrap, or fabric.

cellophane: a thin, transparent paper available in sheets or rolls and in a variety of colors.

composition gold leaf: a metal alloy that comes in thin, 5-inch-square sheets, used to gild surfaces; usually adhered using gold size when applied to nonporous surfaces but can be applied to porous surfaces using rubber cement. Also called Dutch metal.

dry ballpoint pen: a writing implement that no longer has ink, used to emboss or score lines.

etching cream: a thick cream that, when applied to glass, degrades the surface and gives it a frosted appearance.

floral pins: metal pins used to secure flowers or foliage to Styrofoam forms for wreaths and other decorations. Also called greening or U pins.

glitter
glass: fine or coarse transparent glass chips in a variety of colors.
micro or fine: fine or extremely fine flecks made from aluminum or polyester.

gold size: a liquid varnish that is applied with a brush and dries to a high tack for use in adhering gold or silver composition leaf.

hand saw: a small saw held in hand and operated manually.

high-tack white glue: a thick nontoxic white adhesive with a pasty consistency that is used to join porous materials. It dries at faster rate than white glue and usually does not warp paper unless applied in thick coats.

hot-glue gun: a handheld glue dispenser that heats glue sticks and dispenses melted glue through the nozzle.

kraft paper: industrial paper made from wood pulp and resembling brown paper bags. Available in three weights: light, which is best for general craft use and working with materials such as glue or glitter, and medium and heavy, which are more absorbent and should be used when working with liquids like paint or spray adhesive.

mat board: a heavyweight, thick paper whose stiff properties make it ideal for creating a border for a photograph or a structure that supports heavier items like beads.

Mod Podge: a waterbased sealer, glue, and finish that dries with a clear sheen. Used most often for decopage, but also for adhering lables.

monofilament: a single untwisted strand of synthetic material.

needle-nose pliers: a small pincer-type tool with long serrated jaws for gripping small objects and bending wire.

organdy: lightweight sheer fabric often made from cotton.

oven-bake polymer clay: a pliable modeling compound that is cured by baking in a household oven.

paint
acrylic: general-purpose, water-based craft paint. Available in many colors, it is nontoxic and cleans up with soap and water. It can be used on primed or nonporous surfaces.

air-dry transparent glass: designed specifically to paint on glass. It can be dried at room temperature and does not need to be cured by baking.

liquid lead: thick paint that imitates the look of soldering on stained glass. Designed to be applied to nonporous surfaces to be air-dried.

pen: a writing implement that dispenses a steady stream of paint from the tip and allows for more control when applying paint. Perfect for painting small items or for creating detailed areas or words.

spray: water- or oil-based paint contained in an aerosol can that allows quick, even application. Available in both satin and gloss finishes.

paper

medium-weight: paper that bends slightly when stood on end (one-ply chipboard, bristol, cardstock, etc.).

tracing: a lightweight, translucent paper used to mark the lines of a pattern.

rayon velvet: a highly textured fabric that consists of a backing that holds short threads made of rayon. Better suited than cotton velvet to imprinting designs using an embossing method.

ribbon

curling ribbon: crimped paper ribbon, most commonly found in stationery stores, that when run against scissor blades curls up into ringlets.

organdy: lightweight, often very sheer ribbon made from cotton fabric.

satin: soft, smooth ribbon with a high sheen.

tube: manufactured wide ribbon that has been folded and sewn at edge to create a tube.

wire-edged: ribbon with thin copper wire sewn into its edges, which allows ribbon to keep its shape when manipulated.

rubber cement: an adhesive with plasticity and nonwrinkling and noncurling properties, made especially for use on paper.

score: a very narrow groove in paper made by applying pressure with a stylus, X-Acto knife, fork tines, or a dry ballpoint pen against a straightedge ruler used to make folds neat. Paper folds away from a scored mark.

self-adhesive press-type letters: letters and numerals usually made from pliable vinyl.

self-healing mat: a cutting surface made from dense rubber whose cuts close after a blade is passed over the surface, so as to maintain a smooth cutting surface.

spray adhesive: rubber cement dispensed from an aerosol can. It is excellent for laminating paper and fabric and for coating various surfaces to apply glitter.

spray primer: pigment dispensed from an aerosol can that seals a porous surface, providing a ground for additional color or patina material.

stencil: A pattern formed by cutting a shape and printing from the negative space left by the cutout.

Styrofoam: trademark for rigid, lightweight cellular polystyrene. Comes in a variety of shapes and sizes including spheres, rings, and sheets.

tape

floral: narrow, flexible band composed of a paper composite that is tacky and has elastic properties and is used to secure stems of plant material. Available in green, brown, and white.

masking: self-adhesive paper tape that can be removed easily without damaging surfaces.

Ultimate Bond: two-sided plastic tape that can be adhered to ground material while offering an exposed adhesive surface upon which to apply a decorative granular material. Ultimate Bond is a registered trademark of ScottiCrafts.

Teenie Weenie Beadies: small beads without holes, available in many colors, used to create textural and optical effects when applied to paper, fabric, and decorative objects in combination with spray adhesive, Mod Podge, or Ultimate Bond tape. Teenie Weenie Beadies is a registered trademark of ScottiCrafts.

tinsel: thin sheets, strips, or threads of tin or metal foil.

tinsel stem: a length of twisted wire that traps short fibers of cotton or tinsel. Also known as a pipe cleaner.

vellum: a lightweight translucent paper that appears frosted and is often used as an overlay. It is available in three weights: light, medium, and heavy.

wire: a filament of metal whose thickness is measured in gauges. A 30-gauge wire is small and thin; 24-gauge, a medium-width wire; and 16-gauge, a large or thick wire. Usually sold in spools.

wire cutters: a tool with sharp blades used to cut wire of varying gauges.

wire mesh: material woven of metal wires in varying deniers, which indicates how many threads are in a square inch.

X-Acto knife: originally a manufacturer's name and now a common name for a utility knife that has an angled metal blade attached to a cylindrical handle. Blades are available in several styles and thicknesses and are made to be replaced, thereby guaranteeing clean cuts.

Source List

GENERAL CRAFT SUPPLIES

Coffee Break Designs
P.O. Box 34281
Indianapolis, IN 46234
(317) 290-1542
Snaps

Craft King
P.O. Box 90637
Lakeland, Fl 33804
(800) 769-9494

Dick Blick Art Materials
P.O. Box 1267
Galesburg, IL 61402-1267
(800) 447-8192

Impress
120 Andover Park East
Tukwila, WA 98188
(206) 901-9101
Snaps

Pearl Paint Company, Inc
308 Canal Street
New York, N.Y. 10013-2572
(800) 221-6845

Sax Arts & Crafts
P.O. Box 510710
New Berlin, WI 53151-0710
(800) 558-6696

Sunshine Discount Crafts
P.O. Box 301
Largo, Fl 33779-0301
(800) 729-2878
www.sunshinecrafts.com
Teenie Weenie Beadies™,
Ultimate Bond™ Tape

BEADS

Beadworks, Inc.
149 Water Street
Norwalk, CT 06854
(203) 852-9108

Ornamental Resources, Inc.
P.O. Box 3010
1427 Miner Street
Idaho Springs, CO 80452
(800) 876-6762

Toho Shoji
990 Sixth Avenue
New York, N.Y. 10018
(212) 868-7466

FLORAL SUPPLIES

May Silk
16202 Distribution Way
Cerritos, CA 90703
(800) 282-7455

Pany Silk
146 West Twenty-eighth Street
New York, N.Y. 10001
(212) 645-9526
Plastic-coated Styrofoam birds and fruit,
silk flowers

A World of Plenty
P.O. Box 1153
Hermantown, MN 55810-9724
(218) 729-6761

GLITTER

Jones Tones
33865 United Avenue
Pueblo, CO 81001
(800) 397-9667
www.jonestones.com

Martha By Mail
P.O. Box 60060
Tampa, Fl 33660-0060
(800) 950-7130
www.MarthaStewart.com
Glass glitter

SEWING NOTIONS, FABRIC, RIBBON AND TRIM

B&J Fabric
263 West Fortieth Street
New York, N.Y. 10018
(212) 354-8150

M&J Trim
1008 Sixth Avenue
New York, N.Y. 10018
(212) 391-6200

Mokuba
55 West Thirty-ninth Street
New York, N.Y. 10018
(212) 869-8900
Trim

Patterson Silks
36 East Fourteenth Street
New York, N.Y. 10003
(212) 929-7861

WIRE

Metalliferous
34 West Forty-sixth Street
New York, N.Y. 10036
(888) 944-0909
Wire mesh

Nasco Arts & Crafts
901 Janesville Avenue
P.O. Box 901
Fort Atkinson, WI 53538-0901
(800) 558-9595

patterns

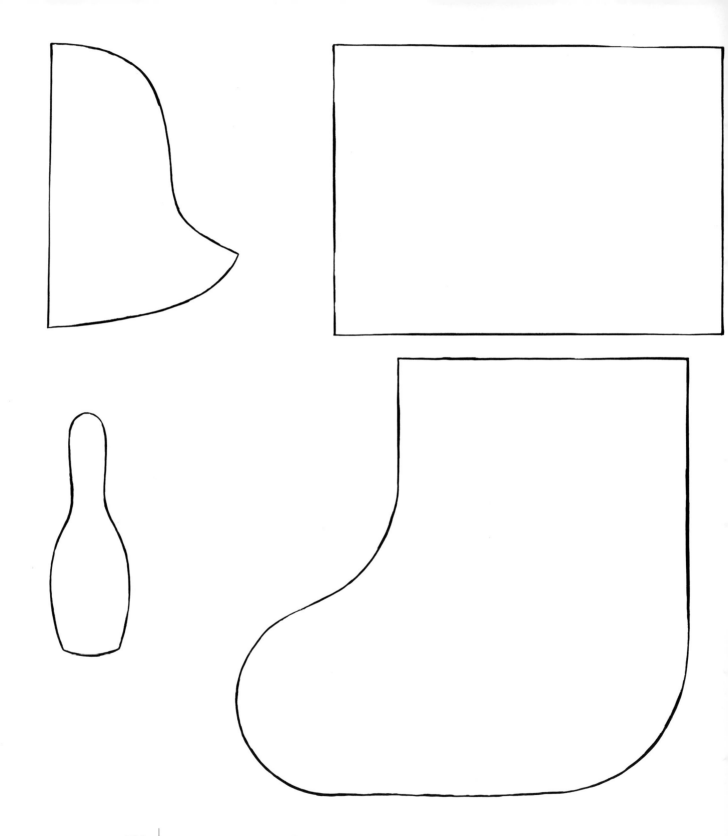

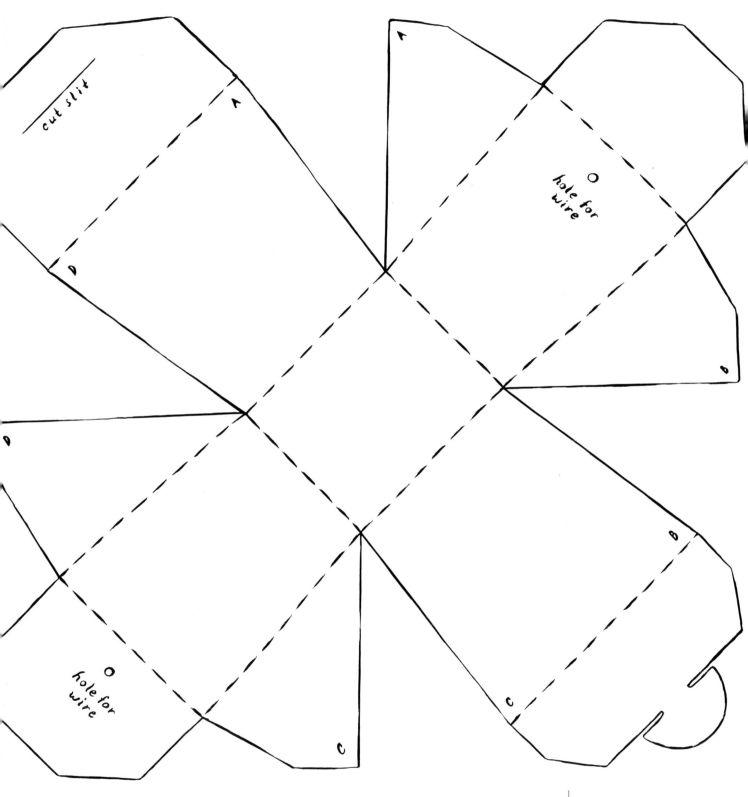

cut slit

hole for
wire

hole for
wire

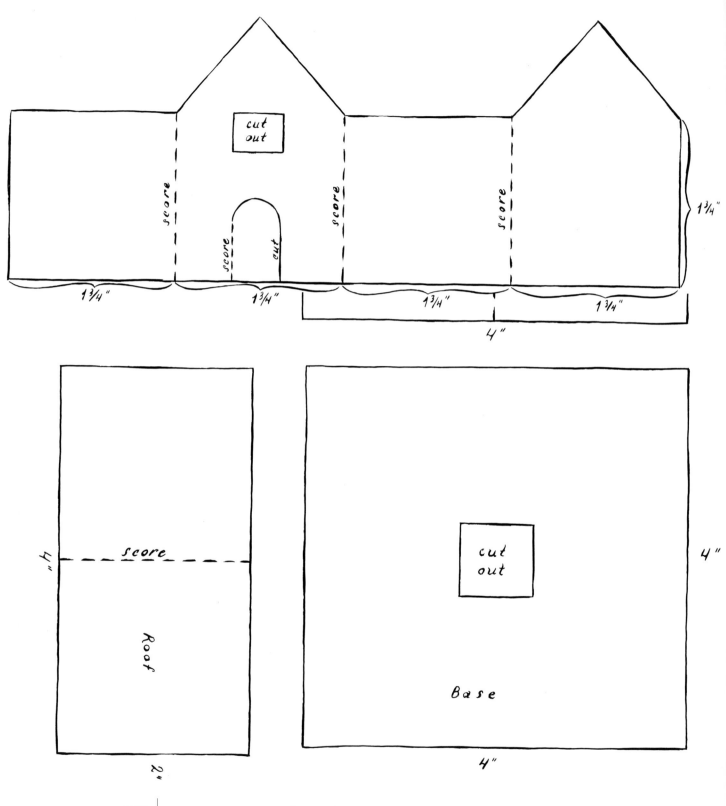

cut
out

score

score

cut

score

score

1¾"

1¾"

1¾"

1¾"

1¾"

4"

4"

score

Roof

2"

cut
out

Base

4"

4"

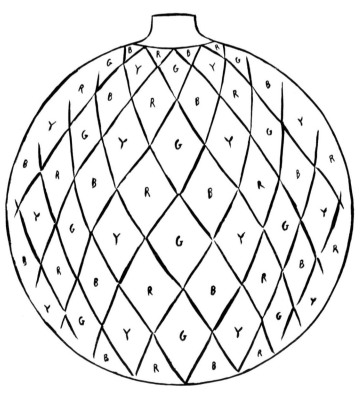

index